Schools
Have Rules

by **Thomas Kingsley Troupe**

illustrated by **Rea Zhai**

PICTURE WINDOW BOOKS
a capstone imprint

HA-JOON

Name: **Ha-Joon**

Birthday: **October 4**

Favorite color: **blue**

Favorite food: **pancakes**

Favorite animal: **elephant**

I want to be a: **teacher**

Table of Contents

What Rules Do

School is where we go to learn. We practice the ABCs and numbers. We learn to read and write. We learn how to make smart choices and be a good friend. Rules keep our classrooms clean and quiet so we can do all of these things. Rules keep us safe. And they make sure everyone at school is treated fairly.

My name's Ha-Joon. Let's take a look at the rules we have at my school.

Raise Your Hand

It's fun to learn new things at school. There's so much to know! My class gets excited—and sometimes loud.

Rule number one: When we want a turn, we raise a hand. Then we wait for our teacher, Mr. Bay, to call on us. Mr. Bay says if we all talk at the same time, no one can learn.

Library Lessons

We have rules to follow in the library too. They help make sure we all have a good time while we're there. When Mrs. Garcia reads a book to us, we sit quietly. No talking! She does really funny voices for the characters.

The best part is taking books home from the library. It's important to take care of the books we borrow. We keep them clean and are careful not to rip the pages. We want the books to be in good shape for the next readers.

YOUR TURN! Why do you think it's important to sit still and listen when someone's reading you a story?

Bathroom Rules

The bathroom rules at school are a lot like the ones at home. To keep the bathroom clean, we flush the toilet when we're done. To keep from spreading germs, we wash our hands. With soap!

Sometimes accidents happen. Anyone can have one. If we have an accident, we let Mr. Bay know right away. He helps us put our dirty clothes in a bag. Be sure to keep extra clothes in your locker!

YOUR TURN! How do you let your teacher know you need to use the bathroom?

11

Be Kind

Some days it's hard to stand or sit still. We do our best to keep our hands and feet to ourselves. I don't like it when kids push me, so I try not to do it to them.

Mr. Bay says it's always best to be kind, no matter where we are. We should treat each other how we want to be treated. He calls that rule the Golden Rule.

Good Manners

Following the Golden Rule is really just having good manners. Be kind. I try to do nice things for the kids in my class. I share. And when I'm nice to others, they're nice to me too!

Once in a while, we might make each other mad. We might say something we don't mean. Bad feelings make it hard for us to learn. Mr. Bay says everyone has bad days. It's OK. When that happens, we say we're sorry and take a time out.

YOUR TURN! Everyone has bad days. What happens when you get mad at school?

15

Time to Eat

I love lunchtime! But we can't go to the lunchroom until we line up straight. That's the rule! In the hallway, there's no talking. Zero. None. We don't want to bother other classes.

He smelled hay and horses. He heard his father's fiddle and the spring peepers. He heard church bells, fire truck bells, the ice cream man's bell, and the train's bell and whistle.

On the Fourth of July, Charlie rode a float. He heard fireworks and his father's band with the big bass drum. He heard the applause, sighs, and cheers of the crowd.

One day, church bells rang during a thunderstorm. "Listen!" said Charlie's father, and dashed out into the downpour. Soaked, he rushed back and struck a cluster of notes on the piano. Thunder rumbled and bells clanged. "That's not *quite* it," he said to Charlie, and again ran into the rain. Dripping, he returned and tried another chord.